AF449512

No part of this work may be reproduced, incorporated into a computer system, or transmitted in any form or by any means (electronic, mechanical, photocopying, recording or otherwise) without the prior written permission of the copyright holders. Infringement of such rights may constitute an intellectual property crime.
Oracle of the Law of Attraction © Grete Stars, 2023

Oracle

of the

Law of

Attraction

⭐ **Grete Stars**

The **Law of Attraction** is a powerful force that attracts to us what we desire or fear. To use it to your advantage:

- Define and **focus on what you "do want"** and not on what you "don't want".
- **Feel, visualize and act** as if what you desire is already part of your reality.

Your **Oracle** will show you the answer you seek and the thought you must focus on to achieve your desire.

Now you can bring together the Power of the Law of Attraction with the Power of the Cosmos and transform your life forever.

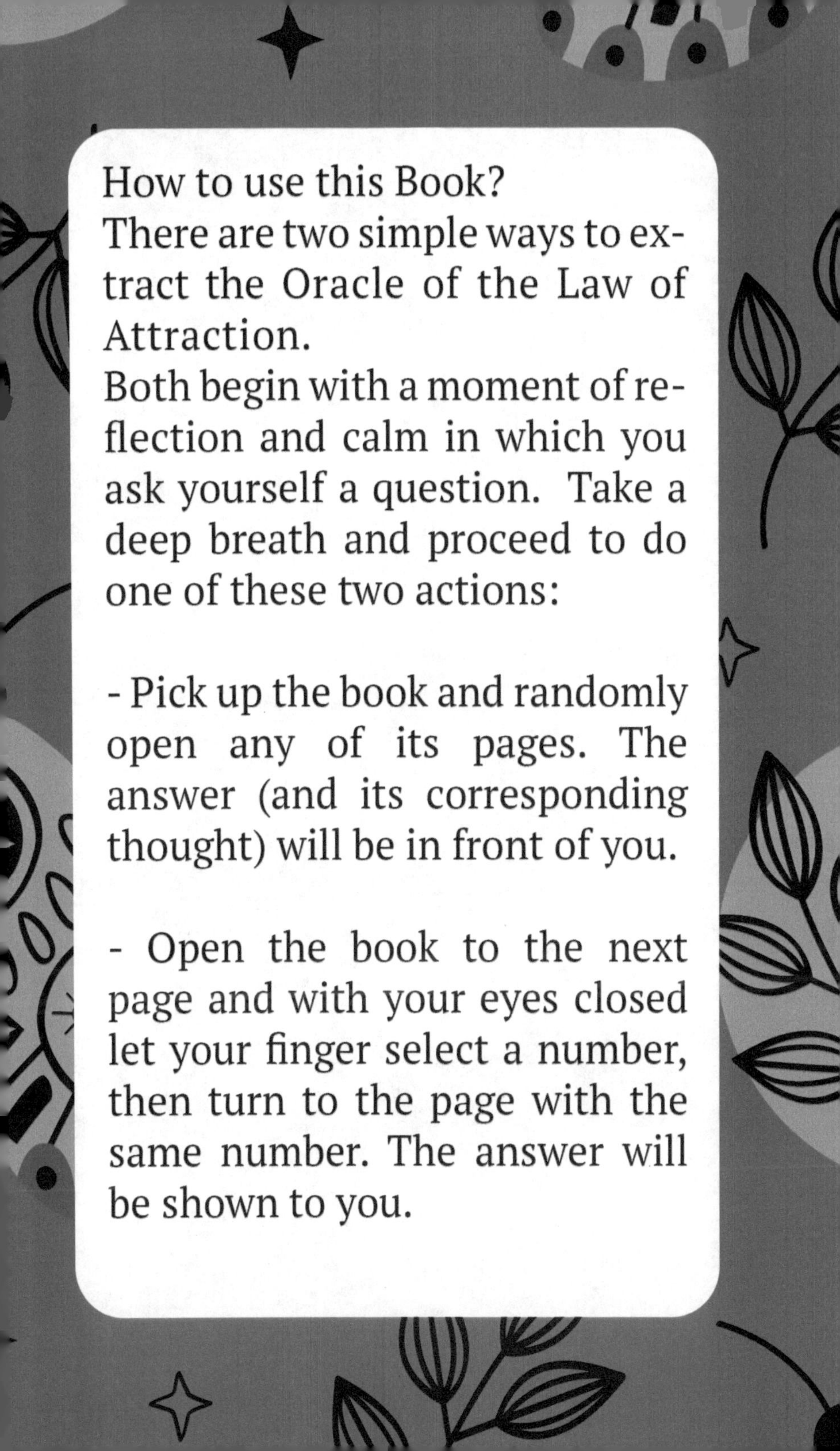

How to use this Book?
There are two simple ways to extract the Oracle of the Law of Attraction.
Both begin with a moment of reflection and calm in which you ask yourself a question. Take a deep breath and proceed to do one of these two actions:

- Pick up the book and randomly open any of its pages. The answer (and its corresponding thought) will be in front of you.

- Open the book to the next page and with your eyes closed let your finger select a number, then turn to the page with the same number. The answer will be shown to you.

Focus on where you want to go, not on what you fear.

You must become aware of your thoughts, you must choose your thoughts carefully, because you are the masterpiece of your own life.

1

If you can't stop thinking about something, don't stop working on it.

Everything I seed in my subconscious mind and nurture with repetition and emotion will one day become a reality.

2

You are destined for more beautiful peaks. Let it go.

Wealth is not what I have.
It's what I am.

3

It's simple: just make it happen.

I take the first step
with faith.
I don't worry if I can't see
the staircase, I'll just take
the first step.

Don't settle for
what you need,
fight for what
you deserve.

I let the infinite abundance
of the Universe
rain on me.

5

*You must do
what you think
you cannot do.*

I am the energy
I want to attract.

6

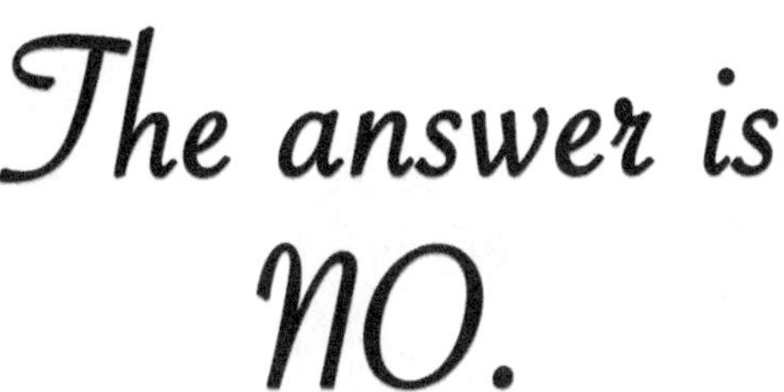

The whole Universe works
in my favor,
I just have to believe it.

Life will give you everything you think you deserve.

Everything I am seeking is seeking me.

8

There is something in you that the World needs. Move forward without hesitation.

I choose to be positive.
I have that choice,
I own my attitude.
Optimism is the thread
to success.

9

The moment is not propitious for action but for deep meditation.

The vibration of
my thoughts and emotions
create my reality.

10

A journey of ten thousand miles begins with a single step. Take that step now.

If I see it in my mind,
I will have it in my hands.

Do something today that your future self will thank you for. You already know what it is.

Everything I want is out there waiting for me to ask.
Everything I want is also looking for me.
I just have to take action to get it.

If you are looking for different results, don't do always the same thing.

What I am is what
I have been.
Who I am going to be is
what I do now.

13

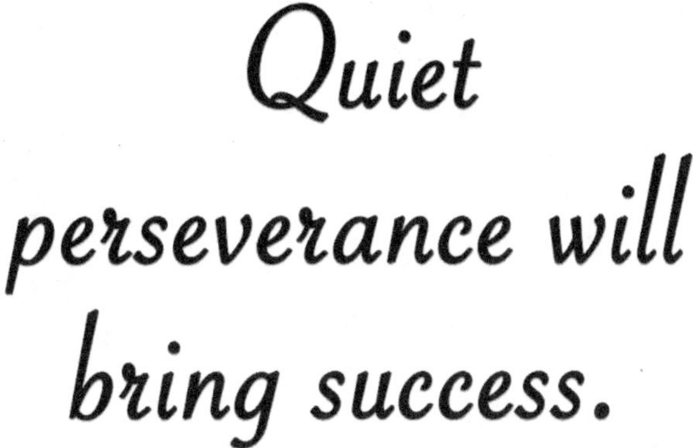

Quiet perseverance will bring success.

Any idea, plan or purpose
can be placed in the mind
through repetition
of the thought.

If the mountain you are climbing seems more and more imposing, it means that the top is getting closer.

If I desire success I must always have the imagination to live, move, think and act as if I have earned that success, or I will never earn it.

15

*Visualize with
all your being
that goal and
act in 3 days.*

There is no limit to what the
Law of Attraction can do for
me, if I dare to believe
in my own vision as
a fact already achieved.

16

No life is complete without a touch of madness. Take a risk.

I follow my happiness
and the Universe
will open doors
where there were walls.

Those who think long and hard before taking a step will spend their whole life on one foot.

Have faith.
Believe in the invisible.

18

*Those who do
not believe in
magic, will never
find it.*

Through thought,
what I desire comes to me.
Through action,
I receive it.

19

Greater achievements are waiting for you.
The answer is NO.

Nature does not hurry,
but it accomplishes
everything.

20

Difficulties do not exist to make you give up but to make you stronger.

We all possess more Power and greater possibilities than we realize.
Visualizing them is one of the greatest powers we have.

21

*If there is
no change,
there are
no butterflies.*

What I resist,
persists.

22

*When was the last time you did something for the first time?
Get off the beaten path.*

Anything my mind
can conceive,
I can achieve.

No.
Set your mind on another goal.

My thoughts lead me to my purposes.
My purposes to my actions.
My actions to my habits.
My habits to my character and my character determines my destiny.

24

It is propitious to move forward in spite of the difficulties.

Everything is in my hands.
No matter where I am now,
no matter what has happened
in my life.
I can begin to consciously
choose my thoughts
and change my life.

25

Don't look for the perfect moment, just find the moment and make it perfect.

If you believe it,
you create it.

26

*Your best teacher is your biggest mistake.
The answer is in the past.*

The key to abundance is to confront limiting experiences with limitless thoughts.

*If not now,
when?*

I give thanks for all
that I receive,
for all the gifts
that come into my life.

28

*Do not
move forward
if you are in
doubt.*

I am a successful and
prosperous person
and the whole Universe
supports me.

29

The scariest moment is always just before you start.
Go for it.

Everything comes into my life at the right time. Everything comes for my greatest blessing.

30

*It seems
impossible until
it is done.*

I receive it, I deserve it,
I bless it with open arms
and I'm ready for more.

You can't play
God without
knowing
the devil well.
It is time
for reflection.

I am a magnet that attracts
happiness, love, health and
prosperity.

32

Take the first step.

I deserve all
the wonderful things that
happen in my life,
I am grateful for them and
I enjoy them.

When in doubt, turn off the noise and listen to your heart.

Love is in me and in every person around me, in every person I talk to and in every person with whom I have contact or establish a relationship.

YES
NO

*If you judge,
you cannot love.
Trust others.*

The wealth of the
Universe is infinite and
manifests itself every day
in my life.

35

You are what
you do, not what
you say you
will do.
The answer is
YES.

My inner world grows, my
prosperity visualizations are
clear and my emotions
vibrate at the
highest frequencies.

36

*Everything you
need to be happy
lies on the other
side of your
fears.*

I feel joy, bliss, happiness,
peace, I am confident that
my desires are aligned with
the Universe.

37

You don't have
to be great
to start.
But you do have
to start in order
to be great.

I have a cheerful and
happy spirit and all
doors are open to me.

*Not everything
that seems to be,
is.*
Caution.

I am grateful to all the
people who teach me
something and enrich
my life.

39

Pessimists see difficulties in every opportunity. Optimists see opportunities in every difficulty. Who do you want to be?

Every day I create my own life, decide my purpose and design the mission for my world and the Universe.

40

NOTES

NOTES 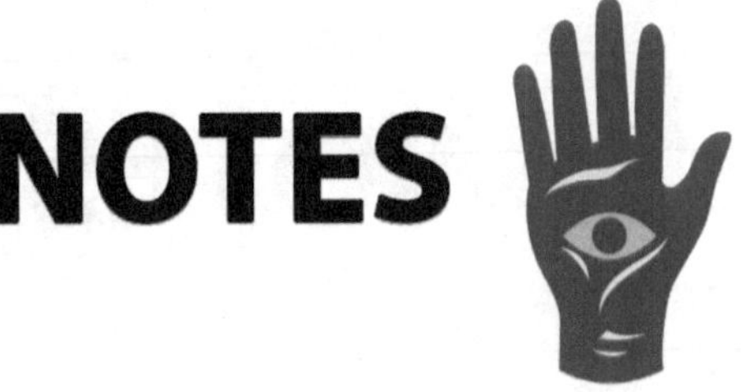

NOTES 

NOTES

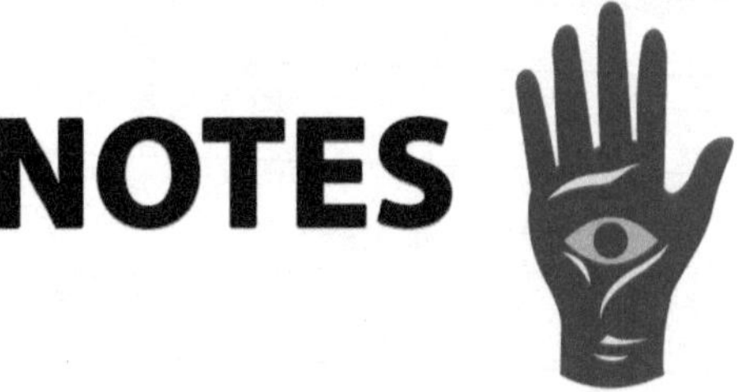

www.ingramcontent.com/pod-product-compliance
Lightning Source LLC
LaVergne TN
LVHW091616170726
843492LV00007B/2438